VERY LITTLE
IS NEEDAD
TO MAKE
A HAPPY LIFE,
IT IS ALL WITHIN
YOURSE LF, IN
YOUR WAY OF
THINKING
..............MARCUS AURELIUS..............

www.ingramcontent.com/pod-product-compliance
Lightning Source LLC
Chambersburg PA
CBHW070126290526
45789CB00005B/2147